DYLAN THOMAS

Derek Mahon was born in Belfast in 1941, studied at Trinity
College, Dublin, and the Sorbonne, and has held journalistic
and academic appointments in London and New York.
A member of Aosdána, he has received numerous awards
including the Irish Academy of Letters Award and the Scott
Moncrieff translation prize. His *Collected Poems* was published
in 1999.

DYLAN THOMAS
Poems selected by DEREK MAHON

faber and faber

First published in 2004
by Faber and Faber Limited
3 Queen Square London WC1N 3AU

Photoset by Wilmaset Ltd, Birkenhead, Wirral
Printed in England by Bookmarque Ltd, Croydon

A CIP record for this book
is available from the British Library

ISBN 0–571–21834–2

10 9 8 7 6 5 4 3 2 1

Contents

Introduction

It's now fifty years since the death of Dylan Thomas. He's by no means a forgotten figure, of course, and certainly not in Wales; but so recurrent and strangely vindictive have been the attacks on his reputation, we might be forgiven for forgetting to take him entirely seriously. Now that most verse is 'light', those who feel poetry has lost touch with some vital function could do worse than read him again. As it happens, recent criticism has recognized what we knew at heart all along – that he was the real thing (despite his own disclaimers), the true vatic voice, if slightly overdone from time to time. We listened entranced to those recordings first time round; though the real work took place on the page. Robert Graves long ago recorded his own response to those famous Welsh BBC tones: 'He could put on the *hwyl*, albeit in English as spoken in Langham Place; and, when I listened to him broadcasting, I had to keep a tight hold of myself to avoid being seduced.' Poetic prodigies are monstrous and ill-omened, he tells us, while conceding that 'the poems show every sign of an alert and sober intelligence'. Graves's own poetic scheme, as summarized in 'To Juan at the Winter Solstice', approves both 'learned bard' and 'gifted child'. Graves himself was the learned bard; Thomas, though remarkably well-read, we may take as a 'gifted child' – in his own famous formulation, 'the Rimbaud of Cwmdonkin Drive', systematically deranged on all the vowels of the rainbow. As for 'monstrous and ill-omened', this is surely unfair to one who started out with such enormous courage and so few advantages. These few were very real, however: a happy childhood; a good education at Swansea Grammar School, where his father was English master; confidence, wit, charm and, of course, native genius. One might also add that, by going from school straight into local theatre and journalism, he instinctively protected his secret, explosive talent from academic discipline and constraint – an advantage he shared with Hardy and Yeats, to name but two. (He thought Yeats the 'best', while Hardy was his 'favourite'.) This remained the pattern. An actor and journalist himself, he preferred actors and journalists to academics who, with some exceptions, scared him stiff. The real thing, he chose like Yeats 'excited reverie' over 'earnest company' and critical theory.

Many still treasure the naive amplitude of the old Dent *Collected Poems* (1952), with its portrait by Augustus John, and cherish a handful of poems there made widely available for the first time: 'The Force that through the Green Fuse Drives the Flower', 'A Refusal to Mourn the Death, by Fire, of a Child in London', 'The Hunchback in the Park', 'Fern Hill', and the one everyone knows, 'Do Not Go Gentle into that Good Night'. Some of the earliest poems, written in his teens, speak still to the adolescent in all of us: 'Before I Knocked', 'Where Once the Waters of Your Face' – body poems, hymns to genetic turmoil. 'The greatest description I know of our earthiness,' he wrote to Pamela Hansford Johnson, 'is to be found in John Donne's *Devotions*, where he describes man as earth of the earth, his body earth, his hair a wild shrub growing out of the land. All thoughts and actions emanate from the body. Every idea, intuitive or intellectual, can be imagined or translated in terms of the body, its flesh, skin, bone, sinews, veins, glands, organs, cells or senses.' A 'receiving station for creaturely intimations', in Seamus Heaney's phrase, he was not only hoping to bed this refined young woman but also in psychosexual revolt against the provincial industrialism of South Wales and, by extension, 'modern civilization' – which he nonetheless enjoyed in the form of comics, thrillers and popular science.

The short stories, echoing Lawrence, take a dim view of the industrial landscape. 'Just Like Little Dogs', in thirties *noir* mode, finds our hero 'listening to the noises from the muffled town, a goods train shunting, a siren in the docks, the hoarse trams in the streets far behind, one bark of a dog, unplaceable sounds, iron being beaten, the distant creaking of wood, doors slamming where there were no houses, an engine coughing like a sheep on a hill'; and this, from 'One Warm Saturday': 'The light from the one weak lamp in a rusty circle fell across the brick-heaps and the broken wood and the dust that had been houses once, where the small and hardly known and never-to-be-forgotten people of the dirty town had lived and loved and died and, always, lost.' An environment from which, in 'Where Tawe Flows', the protagonist dreams of escape: 'It was understood that he would soon be leaving for London to make a career in Chelsea as a free-lance journalist; he was penniless and hoped, in a vague way, to live on women.' Thomas did indeed make a career in Chelsea as a free-lance journalist; also as a screenwriter in Wardour Street and as a brilliant broadcaster in Langham Place, where he impressed and worked with the likes of Louis MacNeice. The speaker in the later 'Return Journey' describes his younger self as 'a bombastic adolescent provincial Bohemian, a gabbling, ambitious, mock-tough, pretentious young man', anxious to be gone.

'I'm not a countryman,' he told Vernon Watkins. 'I stand for, if anything, the aspidistra, the provincial drive, the morning café, the evening pub, hotel and cinema, bookshop and tube station.' But another of his early advantages was, precisely, a strong rural connection through his parents' Welsh-speaking country background. He lived at different times in many different places (many of the 'right' places, you might say): Fitzrovia, Chelsea, Oxford, Sussex, Dorset and Cornwall, not counting trips to Donegal and Tuscany, a writers' conference in Prague and film work in Teheran where, in need of cash, he researched a promotional feature for the Anglo-Iranian Oil Co. But in a sense, if he left Swansea, he never really left Wales – not rural Carmarthenshire certainly, where an uncle and aunt, Jack and Ann Jones, had their old farm Fern Hill, the scene of his idyllic childhood holidays; and more particularly the seaside, coastal Wales of the Gower Peninsula, New Quay and Laugharne (pron. 'Larne'), where he and Caitlin finally settled. His day in misty-castled Laugharne, reports the stormy but crucial

Caitlin in *Leftover Life to Kill* (1957), consisted of an ostensibly very simple, even 'moronic' existence: mornings in the pub, late lunch and then, 'blown up with muck and somnolence, up to his humble shed nesting high above the estuary, and bang into intensive scribbling' – a tidal rhythm echoed in the ebbing-and-flowing structure of the 'Author's Prologue' specially written for *Collected Poems*.

The poems fall roughly into groups, cycles even: the adolescent, 'surrealist' and wartime poems; poems of love and marriage; birthday poems and elegies; and finally the tantalizing, unfinished sequence first projected under the title 'In Country Heaven'. The adolescent and 'surrealist' poems were, astonishingly, written or at least drafted between the ages of seventeen and twenty. Bursting with testosterone and oestrogen, some frankly onanistic, they shocked and intrigued his first readers in equal measure. The usual euphemism was 'visceral'. The unborn speak; much of the action takes place in the womb; vagina and foetus are everywhere in 'obscure' paraphrase, sexual frustration and confusion never far away (but that's life) in poems like 'I See the Boys of Summer' and the still extraordinary, renegade-Christian 'Before I Knocked', a defining moment in the poetry of the time, the 'Jesus poem' about incarnation, spirit and flesh:

> As yet ungotten, I did suffer;
> The rack of dreams my lily bones
> Did twist into a living cipher,
> And flesh was snipped to cross the lines
> Of gallow crosses on the liver
> And brambles in the wringing brains.

Registers and motifs of this kind would be picked up by other poets and artists within a few years when the neo-Romantic, 'New Apocalypse' movement got going. The inchoate meanings of the early poems can be, and have been, extensively figured out. What is at issue here is the creative principle itself. 'Light Breaks Where No Sun Shines', for instance, develops the implications of Donne's medieval, indeed immemorial 'stardust' picture of human physique, an idea known to Giordano Bruno and to ancient Egypt. Relatedly, the beautiful 'Where Once the Waters of Your Face' clings to a natural magic under threat of extinction:

> Dry as a tomb, your coloured lids
> Shall not be latched while magic glides
> Sage on the earth and sky;
> There shall be corals in your beds,
> There shall be serpents in your tides,
> Till all our sea-faiths die.

Some of the difficulties facing a new reader derive from the difficulties facing this new and highly original writer in his early days, and a number of these poems ('Should Lanterns Shine', 'I Have Longed to Move Away', 'Once It Was the Colour of Saying', even perhaps the strange, daunting and haunting 'Altarwise by Owl-Light' sequence) are concerned with the perplexities of the creative act itself, perplexities ultimately resolved in the simplest, most moving terms, with 'In My Craft or Sullen Art' – where, in Berkeley's phrase, 'the obvious though amazing truth 'tis no witchcraft to see' (that ideas are fictions) reveals itself to the moonstruck poet who realizes he writes not for glory:

> But for the lovers, their arms
> Round the griefs of the ages,
> Who pay no praise or wages
> Nor heed my craft or art.

His 'maturity' is usually dated to 'After the Funeral' (1939), the first of the great elegies, this one for his aunt Annie Jones of Fern Hill; for this was the death of childhood, and the poem is almost the first in which he gets out of himself and confronts (as he had already done in prose) the external world of personality and society, here the provincial constraint of Ann's 'fist of a face' and her 'room with a stuffed fox and a stale fern'. Soon enough, though, he rises to the occasion and, harking back to an older Wales, the 'exuberant bardsmanship' he honoured in Dafydd ap Gwilym, declares himself 'Ann's bard on a raised hearth', and breathes new life into fox and fern. (Thomas loved 'the ferned and foxy woods'; elsewhere we have 'fox light' and, vividly, 'a torch of foxes foams'.) But 'After the Funeral' introduces a new theme, one destined to be of the first importance: the inadequacy of language to the fact of death, a subject already present in some of the early poems but now seized upon and expanded to tremendous effect during the Second World War and specifically during the London Blitz. His initial response to the war was one of horror and derision ('Dylan-shooting begins; girls hot and stupid for soldiers flock knickerless on the cliff'); but it was the making of him. Strikingly unfit for active service, he turned seriously to radio work and documentary film – inspired, like so many, by the communal wartime spirit.

'A Refusal to Mourn', though refusing the usual consolations, is an intensely religious poem in the vein of Welsh pulpit declamation so often evident in Thomas's work. The Biblical last line, which once aroused much critical puzzlement, is explicable in terms of *Revelation*, chapters 20–21: the first death is the natural one, the second the Day of Judgment which the innocent child will be spared. The real problems lie elsewhere, in the main body of the poem, where the details are by no means clear. A naive first reader, like oneself at sixteen, will be thrown initially by Thomas's exiguous punctuation, a standard feature of the poems and one quite easily and impertinently clarified by punctuating the verse for oneself so that, fitted out with hyphens and commas to be immediately readable, the 'Refusal' would begin:

Never until the mankind-making,
Bird-, beast- and flower-
Fathering and all-humbling darkness
Tells with silence the last light breaking

And the still hour
Is come, of the sea tumbling in harness ...

When a house fills with smoke in 'A Child's Christmas in Wales', the fire brigade is called; also Ernie Jenkins because he 'likes fires'. Poets love explosions, said Auden mischievously; and the Blitz, frightful in itself, provoked a remarkable range of artistic response: Elizabeth Bowen's best fiction, Eliot's 'Little Gidding' and MacNeice's incendiary 'Brother Fire'; a renewed interest in music; the graphics of Paul Nash and Henry Moore. There's much to be said, indeed, for looking at Thomas in the cultural context of the period. Art and music mattered to him. 'Ceremony After a Fire Raid' is organ music, 'Fern Hill' a picture by Marc Chagall. The poetic 'New Apocalypse' and the neo-Romantic movement in art responded to the same impulses; the countryside, largely overlooked by the urbane Marxists of the thirties ('the idiocy of rural life'), was rediscovered. This coincided with Thomas's own rediscovery of Wales and issued in some of his finest work.

The love-and-marriage poems have been curiously neglected, perhaps because he published few 'love poems' as the term is generally understood, though his whole work is a love poem. 'Love in the Asylum' has been virtually ignored, and 'The Hunchback in the Park', one of his greatest triumphs, admired for its circumstantial detail though it too is a love poem – for the creative dream, the imagined girl, the Muse herself, 'a woman figure without fault' who watches over the darkness. 'Into Her Lying Down Head' and 'A Winter's Tale', also oddly neglected, perhaps for reasons of tact, are love poems too, Caitlin poems, and form a curious pair, like Dylan and Caitlin themselves. Photographs show her to have been a singularly gorgeous young woman (the Macnamaras of Co. Clare were known for their star quality); but her married life wasn't easy. What began as love-in-a-cottage ended up as love-in-a-mist. While Dylan was off carousing in London with the afternoon men and women of Hangover Square, and later in

New York, she raised three children in their fairly isolated Boat House, beset by solitude and financial problems. 'Into Her Lying Down Head' is about marital infidelities, real or imagined, and isolation (though Laugharne, like St Ives and Kinsale, is now a popular tourist spot); while 'A Winter's Tale', more love story than lyric in structure, resolves all difficulties, all needs, in a fairy-tale nature eroticism owing much, significantly, to traditional biomorphic 'Celtic' imagery: the 'carved mouths in the rock are wind swept strings', blackbirds 'like priests in the cloaked hedge row', thickets 'antlered like deer'. This fine and substantial poem of 135 lines has been largely disregarded too, perhaps for its too obviously picturesque and sentimental touches, perhaps for its calm mystery, its uncharacteristic quietude, its absence of verbal fun and games. Those in favour of mature sexuality, however, will find it celebrated here:

> Burning in the bride bed of love, in the whirl-
> Pool at the wanting centre, in the folds
> Of paradise, in the spun bud of the world.
> And she rose with him flowering in her melting snow.

The more autobiographical birthday poems of these years contain many fine things, even if some have the air of diary entries, extensive notes to himself in preparation for something larger. These aren't the self-regarding exercises some have taken them for, but objective sketches of Laugharne as seen from the 'house on stilts' and the writing shed, of tidal activity and bird life: 'finches fly', herons 'spire and spear'. Conscious of approaching middle age (it's been suggested that he died 'of middle age', though some thought he was just getting into his stride) and a need to enlarge his scope, he concentrated his considerable resources on a new, ambitious, post-war project; and then his revered father died. Heaney has written movingly about the 'almost sobbing counterpoint' of 'Do Not Go Gentle': 'This is a son comforting a father; also, conceivably, the neophyte addressing the legend, the green fuse addressing the burnt-out case'; and he invokes, in relation to Dylan, the myth of Orpheus, who also charmed the birds from the trees yet came to grief in the end. The Orphic voice is there certainly; so too, increasingly, is the Dionysian. This had the legendary tragic outcome ('a bad end, thank God'), as in 'the road to ruin I must run'; but also a festive potential which empowered the last poems and the improvisational, light-weight but historically interesting 'play for voices', *Under Milk Wood*, with its Finneganese night music, its comic polyphony and now quaint period detail. He knew, it goes without saying, his mystical Vaughan and his baroque Milton, while relishing the more endearing eccentricities of lower-middle-class life. The early stories – 'The Burning Baby', 'The School for Witches' – are Gothic, counter-Reformation ima-ginings which surface again, transfigured, in the natural magic of the last poems; his historical reach was a long one.

Thomas had a knack for titles when he chose: *The Map of Love* (1939), *Deaths and Entrances* (1946). After the war he started planning a long poem or sequence, perhaps a volume, to be entitled *In Country Heaven*. He himself understood the dynamics of such enterprises. 'Grandiose schemes are built in order that they may be dropped,' he said, going on to add that, with luck, there might emerge shorter poems of greater weight and depth 'than all the unwritten greatness'; and that's exactly what happened in this instance. The project imagined a world blown to bits by nuclear disaster, with the lost human race looking down from above and remembering life on earth: 'places, fears, love, exultation, misery, animal joy, ignorance and mysteries, all *we* know and do not know'. It will become, he hopes, 'an affirmation of the beautiful and terrible worth of the earth, a praise of what is and could be on this lump in the skies'. Of this 'grandiose' scheme three substantial poems survive: in order of composition, 'In Country Sleep', 'Over Sir John's Hill' and 'In the White Giant's Thigh'. Though perhaps less popular than some of the more immediately dramatic lyrics, these represent his crowning achievement. A trilogy complete in itself, syllogistic in form, the sequence moves from a vision of peace and refuge (a prayer for his daughter Aeronwy asleep in Laugharne) to the menacing external world (whatever is predatory and destructive), and concludes in an ecstasy of rhapsodic resolution and celebration. Laugharne represented for this nature visionary, said Vernon Watkins, 'the last refuge of life and sanity in a nightmare world, the last irregular protest against the regularity and symmetry of madness'. His theme was that of a sacramental universe, the unity of creation. All plants and animals ('thick as thieves'), birds, beasts and flowers, the lake that 'harps to a hail stone', figured in this ecological conception ('Sanctum sanctorum the animal eye of the wood'; 'the rain telling its beads'), as did the precious human singularity comically recorded, as if for a too solemn posterity, in *Under Milk Wood*.

Reality withdraws from technology, even from the microphone. 'Over Sir John's Hill', the most anxious and contrived of the three, also set in Laugharne, is continuous with the Blitz poems in as much as the 'cold war' was immediately continuous with the defeat of Germany and Japan. It was a short step from the East End 'slum of fire' to the destruction of Dresden, the atomic era and the photogenic obliteration of Hiroshima and Nagasaki, a geopolitical script spectrally implicit in Thomas's amateur ornithology ('the birds watch *me*,' he said). His friends the priestly heron and crane are here; but 'the hawk on fire', in its 'hoisted cloud', is what he focuses on as it threatens 'the small birds of the bay' with their 'breast of whistles'. A lover of *Paradise Lost*, as of all lost Edens, he sometimes seems to have lived imaginatively in the seventeenth century. A 'cavalier roundhead', in Paul Durcan's phrase, he was still fighting a private war between the medieval and modern worlds – whence perhaps the religious intensity, even when consciously satirical, everywhere in the work from 'Before I Knocked' to 'In the White Giant's Thigh', that feminized re-working of Shakespeare's 73rd sonnet with its well-known line about the dissolution of the monasteries, 'Bare ruin'd choirs where late the sweet birds sang'. Feminist critics generally praise this poem for its affirmation of female sexuality, quoting Julia Kristeva on 'biological thought'. The 'big girls', the Gwyneths and Rhiannons of the early prose, come into their own here as 'daughters of darkness' in the archaic night, though curiously we're not in Wales but in Dorset, near Caitlin's mother's house. The white giant is the phallic, 200 foot prehistoric figure cut into the 'high chalk hill' of Cerne Abbas, where the poet walks after dark in the 'gigantic glade' as if in a graveyard; though it *is* a sort of Wales since the ancient figure dates from pre-Roman, Celtic times. Much of the incidental detail of the buried women's lives is 'Welsh' too in 'Fern Hill' mode:

> The dust of their kettles and clocks swings to and fro
> Where the hay rides now or the bracken kitchens rust
> As the arc of the billhooks that flashed the hedges low
> And cut the birds' boughs that the minstrel sap ran red.
> They from houses where the harvest kneels, hold me hard,
> Who heard the tall bell sail down the Sundays of the dead
> And the rain wring out its tongues on the faded yard.

The anglocentric hostility this 'dog among the fairies' once aroused has largely evaporated. The legend, inaugurated by John Malcolm Brinnin's *Dylan Thomas in America* (1956) and consolidated by Constantine FitzGibbon's *The Life of Dylan Thomas* (1965), lives on. The hectic alcoholism and premature death fifty years ago at the age of thirty-nine (precipitated by the exhaustion of pitiless reading schedules, crippling anxieties, the treacherous potency of American booze, and the notorious morphine overdose in a New York hospital) ensure that the legend survives along with the work, helped in great measure by the pop-cultural influence of the Beats, the hero worship of self-styled Bob Dylan and even the death from heroin of Sid Vicious – who also spent serious time at the Chelsea Hotel on West 23rd Street: a haven, then as now, for musicians, artists and writers. There's a certain logic in this. Thomas, the hero of a million solitary teenage bedrooms and himself a subversive folk-rock Dionysian celebrity before the concept was co-opted and institutionalized, struck an immediate chord with the young: a proto-feminist and radical pacifist, he talked the talk and walked the walk. Still, it's hard to know who to compare him with in international terms, if such comparisons need be made. Hart Crane perhaps, the Rimbaud of Cleveland, Ohio, with whom he shared a high-strung metaphorical density and an aspiration to over-arching schemes. But I'd like to propose another, unlikely and in most ways antithetical figure (Dylan was anything but diplomatic), a fellow contributor to Marguerite Caetani's once renowned magazine *Botteghe Oscure*. I mean the later Saint-John Perse, another student of Rimbaud, wind, hail, rain and snow; of birds, sea-light and oceanic forces, the prospects of the sea. When the French poet writes that birds, 'conceived by a first inflection and destined for long resonance, move like words to a cosmic rhythm, inscribing themselves instinctively in the great vagrant poem of the evolving earth', he's on the same planet as Dylan Thomas. Disoriented, impenitent, 'dying of strangers', Thomas left us a faith in unfashionable notions like inspiration and genius; also a poetry not of diminished but of enhanced expectation – in his own words, a contribution to reality: 'The world is never the same once a good poem has been added to it. A good poem helps to change the shape and significance of the universe.'

DEREK MAHON

DYLAN THOMAS

Author's Prologue

This day winding down now
At God speeded summer's end
In the torrent salmon sun,
In my seashaken house
On a breakneck of rocks
Tangled with chirrup and fruit,
Froth, flute, fin and quill
At a wood's dancing hoof,
By scummed, starfish sands
With their fishwife cross
Gulls, pipers, cockles, and sails,
Out there, crow black, men
Tackled with clouds, who kneel
To the sunset nets,
Geese nearly in heaven, boys
Stabbing, and herons, and shells
That speak seven seas,
Eternal waters away
From the cities of nine
Days' night whose towers will catch
In the religious wind
Like stalks of tall, dry straw,
At poor peace I sing
To you strangers (though song
Is a burning and crested act,
The fire of birds in
The world's turning wood,
For my sawn, splay sounds),
Out of these seathumbed leaves
That will fly and fall
Like leaves of trees and as soon
Crumble and undie
Into the dogdayed night.

Seaward the salmon, sucked sun slips,
And the dumb swans drub blue
My dabbed bay's dusk, as I hack
This rumpus of shapes
For you to know
How I, a spinning man,
Glory also this star, bird
Roared, sea born, man torn, blood blest.
Hark: I trumpet the place,
From fish to jumping hill! Look:
I build my bellowing ark
To the best of my love
As the flood begins,
Out of the fountainhead
Of fear, rage red, manalive,
Molten and mountainous to stream
Over the wound asleep
Sheep white hollow farms

To Wales in my arms.
Hoo, there, in castle keep,
You king singsong owls, who moonbeam
The flickering runs and dive
The dingle furred deer dead!
Huloo, on plumbed bryns,
O my ruffled ring dove
In the hooting, nearly dark
With Welsh and reverent rook,
Coo rooing the woods' praise,
Who moons her blue notes from her nest
Down the curlew herd!
Ho, hullaballoing clan
Agape, with woe
In your beaks, on the gabbing capes!
Heigh, on horseback hill, jack
Whisking hare! who

Hears, there, this fox light, my flood ship's
Clangour as I hew and smite
(A clash of anvils for my
Hubbub and fiddle, this tune
On a tongued puffball)
But animals thick as thieves
On God's rough tumbling grounds
(Hail to His beasthood!).
Beasts who sleep good and thin,
Hist, in hogsback woods! The haystacked
Hollow farms in a throng
Of waters cluck and cling,
And barnroofs cockcrow war!
O kingdom of neighbours, finned
Felled and quilled, flash to my patch
Work ark and the moonshine
Drinking Noah of the bay,
With pelt, and scale, and fleece:
Only the drowned deep bells
Of sheep and churches noise
Poor peace as the sun sets
And dark shoals every holy field.
We will ride out alone, and then,
Under the stars of Wales,
Cry, Multitudes of arks! Across
The water lidded lands,
Manned with their loves they'll move,
Like wooden islands, hill to hill.
Huloo, my prowed dove with a flute!
Ahoy, old, sea-legged fox,
Tom tit and Dai mouse!
My ark sings in the sun
At God speeded summer's end
And the flood flowers now.

I See the Boys of Summer

I

I see the boys of summer in their ruin
Lay the gold tithings barren,
Setting no store by harvest, freeze the soils;
There in their heat the winter floods
Of frozen loves they fetch their girls,
And drown the cargoed apples in their tides.

These boys of light are curdlers in their folly,
Sour the boiling honey;
The jacks of frost they finger in the hives;
There in the sun the frigid threads
Of doubt and dark they feed their nerves;
The signal moon is zero in their voids.

I see the summer children in their mothers
Split up the brawned womb's weathers,
Divide the night and day with fairy thumbs;
There in the deep with quartered shades
Of sun and moon they paint their dams
As sunlight paints the shelling of their heads.

I see that from these boys shall men of nothing
Stature by seedy shifting,
Or lame the air with leaping from its heats;
There from their hearts the dogdayed pulse
Of love and light bursts in their throats.
O see the pulse of summer in the ice.

II

But seasons must be challenged or they totter
Into a chiming quarter
Where, punctual as death, we ring the stars;

There, in his night, the black-tongued bells
The sleepy man of winter pulls,
Nor blows back moon-and-midnight as she blows.

We are the dark deniers, let us summon
Death from a summer woman,
A muscling life from lovers in their cramp,
From the fair dead who flush the sea
The bright-eyed worm on Davy's lamp,
And from the planted womb the man of straw.

We summer boys in this four-winded spinning,
Green of the seaweeds' iron,
Hold up the noisy sea and drop her birds,
Pick the world's ball of wave and froth
To choke the deserts with her tides,
And comb the county gardens for a wreath.

In spring we cross our foreheads with the holly,
Heigh ho the blood and berry,
And nail the merry squires to the trees;
Here love's damp muscle dries and dies,
Here break a kiss in no love's quarry.
O see the poles of promise in the boys.

III

I see you boys of summer in your ruin.
Man in his maggot's barren.
And boys are full and foreign in the pouch.
I am the man your father was.
We are the sons of flint and pitch.
O see the poles are kissing as they cross.

When Once the Twilight Locks No Longer

When once the twilight locks no longer
Locked in the long worm of my finger
Nor damned the sea that sped about my fist,
The mouth of time sucked, like a sponge,
The milky acid on each hinge,
And swallowed dry the waters of the breast.

When the galactic sea was sucked
And all the dry seabed unlocked,
I sent my creature scouting on the globe,
That globe itself of hair and bone
That, sewn to me by nerve and brain,
Had stringed my flask of matter to his rib.

My fuses timed to charge his heart,
He blew like powder to the light
And held a little sabbath with the sun,
But when the stars, assuming shape,
Drew in his eyes the straws of sleep,
He drowned his father's magics in a dream.

All issue armoured, of the grave,
The redhaired cancer still alive,
The cataracted eyes that filmed their cloth;
Some dead undid their bushy jaws,
And bags of blood let out their flies;
He had by heart the Christ-cross-row of death.

Sleep navigates the tides of time;
The dry Sargasso of the tomb
Gives up its dead to such a working sea;
And sleep rolls mute above the beds
Where fishes' food is fed the shades
Who periscope through flowers to the sky.

When once the twilight screws were turned,
And mother milk was stiff as sand,
I sent my own ambassador to light;
By trick or chance he fell asleep
And conjured up a carcass shape
To rob me of my fluids in his heart.

Awake, my sleeper, to the sun,
A worker in the morning town,
And leave the poppied pickthank where he lies;
The fences of the light are down,
All but the briskest riders thrown,
And worlds hang on the trees.

Before I Knocked

Before I knocked and flesh let enter,
With liquid hands tapped on the womb,
I who was shapeless as the water
That shaped the Jordan near my home
Was brother to Mnetha's daughter
And sister to the fathering worm.

I who was deaf to spring and summer,
Who knew not sun nor moon by name,
Felt thud beneath my flesh's armour,
As yet was in a molten form,
The leaden stars, the rainy hammer
Swung by my father from his dome.

I knew the message of the winter,
The darted hail, the childish snow,
And the wind was my sister suitor;
Wind in me leaped, the hellborn dew;
My veins flowed with the Eastern weather;
Ungotten I knew night and day.

As yet ungotten, I did suffer;
The rack of dreams my lily bones
Did twist into a living cipher,
And flesh was snipped to cross the lines
Of gallow crosses on the liver
And brambles in the wringing brains.

My throat knew thirst before the structure
Of skin and vein around the well
Where words and water make a mixture
Unfailing till the blood runs foul;
My heart knew love, my belly hunger;
I smelt the maggot in my stool.

And time cast forth my mortal creature
To drift or drown upon the seas
Acquainted with the salt adventure
Of tides that never touch the shores.
I who was rich was made the richer
By sipping at the vine of days.

I, born of flesh and ghost, was neither
A ghost nor man, but mortal ghost.
And I was struck down by death's feather.
I was a mortal to the last
Long breath that carried to my father
The message of his dying christ.

You who bow down at cross and altar,
Remember me and pity Him
Who took my flesh and bone for armour
And doublecrossed my mother's womb.

The Force that through the Green Fuse
Drives the Flower

The force that through the green fuse drives the flower
Drives my green age; that blasts the roots of trees
Is my destroyer.
And I am dumb to tell the crooked rose
My youth is bent by the same wintry fever.

The force that drives the water through the rocks
Drives my red blood; that dries the mouthing streams
Turns mine to wax.
And I am dumb to mouth unto my veins
How at the mountain spring the same mouth sucks.

The hand that whirls the water in the pool
Stirs the quicksand; that ropes the blowing wind
Hauls my shroud sail.
And I am dumb to tell the hanging man
How of my clay is made the hangman's lime.

The lips of time leech to the fountain head;
Love drips and gathers, but the fallen blood
Shall calm her sores.
And I am dumb to tell a weather's wind
How time has ticked a heaven round the stars.

And I am dumb to tell the lover's tomb
How at my sheet goes the same crooked worm.

My Hero Bares His Nerves

My hero bares his nerves along my wrist
That rules from wrist to shoulder,
Unpacks the head that, like a sleepy ghost,
Leans on my mortal ruler,
The proud spine spurning turn and twist.

And these poor nerves so wired to the skull
Ache on the lovelorn paper
I hug to love with my unruly scrawl
That utters all love hunger
And tells the page the empty ill.

My hero bares my side and sees his heart
Tread, like a naked Venus,
The beach of flesh, and wind her bloodred plait;
Stripping my loin of promise,
He promises a secret heat.

He holds the wire from his box of nerves
Praising the mortal error
Of birth and death, the two sad knaves of thieves,
And the hunger's emperor;
He pulls the chain, the cistern moves.

Where Once the Waters of Your Face

Where once the waters of your face
Spun to my screws, your dry ghost blows,
The dead turns up its eye;
Where once the mermen through your ice
Pushed up their hair, the dry wind steers
Through salt and root and roe.

Where once your green knots sank their splice
Into the tided cord, there goes
The green unraveller,
His scissors oiled, his knife hung loose
To cut the channels at their source
And lay the wet fruits low.

Invisible, your clocking tides
Break on the lovebeds of the weeds;
The weed of love's left dry;
There round about your stones the shades
Of children go who, from their voids,
Cry to the dolphined sea.

Dry as a tomb, your coloured lids
Shall not be latched while magic glides
Sage on the earth and sky;
There shall be corals in your beds,
There shall be serpents in your tides,
Till all our sea-faiths die.

If I Were Tickled by the Rub of Love

If I were tickled by the rub of love,
A rooking girl who stole me for her side,
Broke through her straws, breaking my bandaged string,
If the red tickle as the cattle calve
Still set to scratch a laughter from my lung,
I would not fear the apple nor the flood
Nor the bad blood of spring.

Shall it be male or female? say the cells,
And drop the plum like fire from the flesh.
If I were tickled by the hatching hair,
The winging bone that sprouted in the heels,
The itch of man upon the baby's thigh,
I would not fear the gallows nor the axe
Nor the crossed sticks of war.

Shall it be male or female? say the fingers
That chalk the walls with green girls and their men.
I would not fear the muscling-in of love
If I were tickled by the urchin hungers
Rehearsing heat upon a raw-edged nerve.
I would not fear the devil in the loin
Nor the outspoken grave.

If I were tickled by the lovers' rub
That wipes away not crow's-foot nor the lock
Of sick old manhood on the fallen jaws,
Time and the crabs and the sweethearting crib
Would leave me cold as butter for the flies,
The sea of scums could drown me as it broke
Dead on the sweethearts' toes.

This world is half the devil's and my own,
Daft with the drug that's smoking in a girl
And curling round the bud that forks her eye.

An old man's shank one-marrowed with my bone,
And all the herrings smelling in the sea,
I sit and watch the worm beneath my nail
Wearing the quick away.

And that's the rub, the only rub that tickles.
The knobbly ape that swings along his sex
From damp love-darkness and the nurse's twist
Can never raise the midnight of a chuckle,
Nor when he finds a beauty in the breast
Of lover, mother, lovers, or his six
Feet in the rubbing dust.

And what's the rub? Death's feather on the nerve?
Your mouth, my love, the thistle in the kiss?
My Jack of Christ born thorny on the tree?
The words of death are dryer than his stiff,
My wordy wounds are printed with your hair.
I would be tickled by the rub that is:
Man be my metaphor.

Our Eunuch Dreams

I

Our eunuch dreams, all seedless in the light,
Of light and love, the tempers of the heart,
Whack their boys' limbs,
And, winding-footed in their shawl and sheet,
Groom the dark brides, the widows of the night
Fold in their arms.

The shades of girls, all flavoured from their shrouds,
When sunlight goes are sundered from the worm,
The bones of men, the broken in their beds,
By midnight pulleys that unhouse the tomb.

II

In this our age the gunman and his moll,
Two one-dimensioned ghosts, love on a reel,
Strange to our solid eye,
And speak their midnight nothings as they swell;
When cameras shut they hurry to their hole
Down in the yard of day.

They dance between their arclamps and our skull,
Impose their shots, showing the nights away;
We watch the show of shadows kiss or kill,
Flavoured of celluloid give love the lie.

III

Which is the world? Of our two sleepings, which
Shall fall awake when cures and their itch
Raise up this red-eyed earth?
Pack off the shapes of daylight and their starch,

The sunny gentlemen, the Welshing rich,
Or drive the night-geared forth.

The photograph is married to the eye,
Grafts on its bride one-sided skins of truth;
The dream has sucked the sleeper of his faith
That shrouded men might marrow as they fly.

IV

This is the world: the lying likeness of
Our strips of stuff that tatter as we move
Loving and being loth;
The dream that kicks the buried from their sack
And lets their trash be honoured as the quick.
This is the world. Have faith.

For we shall be a shouter like the cock,
Blowing the old dead back; our shots shall smack
The image from the plates;
And we shall be fit fellows for a life,
And who remain shall flower as they love,
Praise to our faring hearts.

Especially When the October Wind

Especially when the October wind
With frosty fingers punishes my hair,
Caught by the crabbing sun I walk on fire
And cast a shadow crab upon the land,
By the sea's side, hearing the noise of birds,
Hearing the raven cough in winter sticks,
My busy heart who shudders as she talks
Sheds the syllabic blood and drains her words.

Shut, too, in a tower of words, I mark
On the horizon walking like the trees
The wordy shapes of women, and the rows
Of the star-gestured children in the park.
Some let me make you of the vowelled beeches,
Some of the oaken voices, from the roots
Of many a thorny shire tell you notes,
Some let me make you of the water's speeches.

Behind a pot of ferns the wagging clock
Tells me the hour's word, the neural meaning
Flies on the shafted disk, declaims the morning
And tells the windy weather in the cock.
Some let me make you of the meadow's signs;
The signal grass that tells me all I know
Breaks with the wormy winter through the eye.
Some let me tell you of the raven's sins.

Especially when the October wind
(Some let me make you of autumnal spells,
The spider-tongued, and the loud hill of Wales)
With fists of turnips punishes the land,
Some let me make you of the heartless words.

The heart is drained that, spelling in the scurry
Of chemic blood, warned of the coming fury.
By the sea's side hear the dark-vowelled birds.

In the Beginning

In the beginning was the three-pointed star,
One smile of light across the empty face;
One bough of bone across the rooting air,
The substance forked that marrowed the first sun;
And, burning ciphers on the round of space,
Heaven and hell mixed as they spun.

In the beginning was the pale signature,
Three-syllabled and starry as the smile;
And after came the imprints on the water,
Stamp of the minted face upon the moon;
The blood that touched the crosstree and the grail
Touched the first cloud and left a sign.

In the beginning was the mounting fire
That set alight the weathers from a spark,
A three-eyed, red-eyed spark, blunt as a flower;
Life rose and spouted from the rolling seas,
Burst in the roots, pumped from the earth and rock
The secret oils that drive the grass.

In the beginning was the word, the word
That from the solid bases of the light
Abstracted all the letters of the void;
And from the cloudy bases of the breath
The word flowed up, translating to the heart
First characters of birth and death.

In the beginning was the secret brain.
The brain was celled and soldered in the thought
Before the pitch was forking to a sun;
Before the veins were shaking in their sieve,
Blood shot and scattered to the winds of light
The ribbed original of love.

Light Breaks Where No Sun Shines

Light breaks where no sun shines;
Where no sea runs, the waters of the heart
Push in their tides;
And, broken ghosts with glow-worms in their heads,
The things of light
File through the flesh where no flesh decks the bones.

A candle in the thighs
Warms youth and seed and burns the seeds of age;
Where no seed stirs,
The fruit of man unwrinkles in the stars,
Bright as a fig;
Where no wax is, the candle shows its hairs.

Dawn breaks behind the eyes;
From poles of skull and toe the windy blood
Slides like a sea;
Nor fenced, nor staked, the gushers of the sky
Spout to the rod
Divining in a smile the oil of tears.

Night in the sockets rounds,
Like some pitch moon, the limit of the globes;
Day lights the bone;
Where no cold is, the skinning gales unpin
The winter's robes;
The film of spring is hanging from the lids.

Light breaks on secret lots,
On tips of thought where thoughts smell in the rain;
When logics die,
The secret of the soil grows through the eye,
And blood jumps in the sun;
Above the waste allotments the dawn halts.

Ears in the Turrets Hear

Ears in the turrets hear
Hands grumble on the door,
Eyes in the gables see
The fingers at the locks.
Shall I unbolt or stay
Alone till the day I die
Unseen by stranger-eyes
In this white house?
Hands, hold you poison or grapes?

Beyond this island bound
By a thin sea of flesh
And a bone coast,
The land lies out of sound
And the hills out of mind.
No birds or flying fish
Disturbs this island's rest.

Ears in this island hear
The wind pass like a fire,
Eyes in this island see
Ships anchor off the bay.
Shall I run to the ships
With the wind in my hair,
Or stay till the day I die
And welcome no sailor?
Ships, hold you poison or grapes?

Hands grumble on the door,
Ships anchor off the bay,
Rain beats the sand and slates.
Shall I let in the stranger,
Shall I welcome the sailor,
Or stay till the day I die?

Hands of the stranger and holds of the ships,
Hold you poison or grapes?

The Hand that Signed the Paper

The hand that signed the paper felled a city;
Five sovereign fingers taxed the breath,
Doubled the globe of dead and halved a country;
These five kings did a king to death.

The mighty hand leads to a sloping shoulder,
The finger joints are cramped with chalk;
A goose's quill has put an end to murder
That put an end to talk.

The hand that signed the treaty bred a fever,
And famine grew, and locusts came;
Great is the hand that holds dominion over
Man by a scribbled name.

The five kings count the dead but do not soften
The crusted wound nor stroke the brow;
A hand rules pity as a hand rules heaven;
Hands have no tears to flow.

Should Lanterns Shine

Should lanterns shine, the holy face,
Caught in an octagon of unaccustomed light,
Would wither up, and any boy of love
Look twice before he fell from grace.
The features in their private dark
Are formed of flesh, but let the false day come
And from her lips the faded pigments fall,
The mummy cloths expose an ancient breast.

I have been told to reason by the heart,
But heart, like head, leads helplessly;
I have been told to reason by the pulse,
And, when it quickens, alter the actions' pace
Till field and roof lie level and the same
So fast I move defying time, the quiet gentleman
Whose beard wags in Egyptian wind.

I have heard many years of telling,
And many years should see some change.

The ball I threw while playing in the park
Has not yet reached the ground.

I Have Longed to Move Away

I have longed to move away
From the hissing of the spent lie
And the old terrors' continual cry
Growing more terrible as the day
Goes over the hill into the deep sea;
I have longed to move away
From the repetition of salutes,
For there are ghosts in the air
And ghostly echoes on paper,
And the thunder of calls and notes.

I have longed to move away but am afraid;
Some life, yet unspent, might explode
Out of the old lie burning on the ground,
And, crackling into the air, leave me half-blind.
Neither by night's ancient fear,
The parting of hat from hair,
Pursed lips at the receiver,
Shall I fall to death's feather.
By these I would not care to die,
Half convention and half lie.

And Death Shall Have No Dominion

And death shall have no dominion.
Dead men naked they shall be one
With the man in the wind and the west moon;
When their bones are picked clean and the clean bones gone,
They shall have stars at elbow and foot;
Though they go mad they shall be sane,
Though they sink through the sea they shall rise again;
Though lovers be lost love shall not;
And death shall have no dominion.

And death shall have no dominion.
Under the windings of the sea
They lying long shall not die windily;
Twisting on racks when sinews give way,
Strapped to a wheel, yet they shall not break;
Faith in their hands shall snap in two,
And the unicorn evils run them through;
Split all ends up they shan't crack;
And death shall have no dominion.

And death shall have no dominion.
No more may gulls cry at their ears
Or waves break loud on the seashores;
Where blew a flower may a flower no more
Lift its head to the blows of the rain;
Though they be mad and dead as nails,
Heads of the characters hammer through daisies;
Break in the sun till the sun breaks down,
And death shall have no dominion.

from Altarwise by Owl-Light

I

Altarwise by owl-light in the half-way house
The gentleman lay graveward with his furies;
Abaddon in the hangnail cracked from Adam,
And, from his fork, a dog among the fairies,
The atlas-eater with a jaw for news,
Bit out the mandrake with to-morrow's scream.
Then, penny-eyed, that gentleman of wounds,
Old cock from nowheres and the heaven's egg,
With bones unbuttoned to the half-way winds,
Hatched from the windy salvage on one leg,
Scraped at my cradle in a walking word
That night of time under the Christward shelter:
I am the long world's gentleman, he said,
And share my bed with Capricorn and Cancer.

V

And from the windy West came two-gunned Gabriel,
From Jesu's sleeve trumped up the king of spots,
The sheath-decked jacks, queen with a shuffled heart;
Said the fake gentleman in suit of spades,
Black-tongued and tipsy from salvation's bottle.
Rose my Byzantine Adam in the night.
For loss of blood I fell on Ishmael's plain,
Under the milky mushrooms slew my hunger,
A climbing sea from Asia had me down
And Jonah's Moby snatched me by the hair,
Cross-stroked salt Adam to the frozen angel
Pin-legged on pole-hills with a black medusa
By waste seas where the white bear quoted Virgil
And sirens singing from our lady's sea-straw.

When all My Five and Country Senses See

When all my five and country senses see,
The fingers will forget green thumbs and mark
How, through the halfmoon's vegetable eye,
Husk of young stars and handfull zodiac,
Love in the frost is pared and wintered by,
The whispering ears will watch love drummed away
Down breeze and shell to a discordant beach,
And, lashed to syllables, the lynx tongue cry
That her fond wounds are mended bitterly.
My nostrils see her breath burn like a bush.

My one and noble heart has witnesses
In all love's countries, that will grope awake;
And when blind sleep drops on the spying senses,
The heart is sensual, though five eyes break.

After the Funeral
(In memory of Ann Jones)

After the funeral, mule praises, brays,
Windshake of sailshaped ears, muffle-toed tap
Tap happily of one peg in the thick
Grave's foot, blinds down the lids, the teeth in black,
The spittled eyes, the salt ponds in the sleeves,
Morning smack of the spade that wakes up sleep,
Shakes a desolate boy who slits his throat
In the dark of the coffin and sheds dry leaves,
That breaks one bone to light with a judgment clout,
After the feast of tear-stuffed time and thistles
In a room with a stuffed fox and a stale fern,
I stand, for this memorial's sake, alone
In the snivelling hours with dead, humped Ann
Whose hooded, fountain heart once fell in puddles
Round the parched worlds of Wales and drowned each sun
(Though this for her is a monstrous image blindly
Magnified out of praise; her death was a still drop;
She would not have me sinking in the holy
Flood of her heart's fame; she would lie dumb and deep
And need no druid of her broken body).
But I, Ann's bard on a raised hearth, call all
The seas to service that her wood-tongued virtue
Babble like a bellbuoy over the hymning heads,
Bow down the walls of the ferned and foxy woods
That her love sing and swing through a brown chapel,
Bless her bent spirit with four, crossing birds.
Her flesh was meek as milk, but this skyward statue
With the wild breast and blessed and giant skull
Is carved from her in a room with a wet window
In a fiercely mourning house in a crooked year.
I know her scrubbed and sour humble hands
Lie with religion in their cramp, her threadbare

Whisper in a damp word, her wits drilled hollow,
Her fist of a face died clenched on a round pain;
And sculptured Ann is seventy years of stone.
These cloud-sopped, marble hands, this monumental
Argument of the hewn voice, gesture and psalm,
Storm me forever over her grave until
The stuffed lung of the fox twitch and cry Love
And the strutting fern lay seeds on the black sill.

Once It Was the Colour of Saying

Once it was the colour of saying
Soaked my table the uglier side of a hill
With a capsized field where a school sat still
And a black and white patch of girls grew playing;
The gentle seaslides of saying I must undo
That all the charmingly drowned arise to cockcrow and kill.
When I whistled with mitching boys through a reservoir park
Where at night we stoned the cold and cuckoo
Lovers in the dirt of their leafy beds,
The shade of their trees was a word of many shades
And a lamp of lightning for the poor in the dark;
Now my saying shall be my undoing,
And every stone I wind off like a reel.

The Conversation of Prayers

The conversation of prayers about to be said
By the child going to bed and the man on the stairs
Who climbs to his dying love in her high room,
The one not caring to whom in his sleep he will move
And the other full of tears that she will be dead,

Turns in the dark on the sound they know will arise
Into the answering skies from the green ground,
From the man on the stairs and the child by his bed.
The sound about to be said in the two prayers
For the sleep in a safe land and the love who dies

Will be the same grief flying. Whom shall they calm?
Shall the child sleep unharmed or the man be crying?
The conversation of prayers about to be said
Turns on the quick and the dead, and the man on the stairs
To-night shall find no dying but alive and warm

In the fire of his care his love in the high room.
And the child not caring to whom he climbs his prayer
Shall drown in a grief as deep as his made grave,
And mark the dark eyed wave, through the eyes of sleep,
Dragging him up the stairs to one who lies dead.

A Refusal to Mourn the Death, by Fire, of a Child in London

Never until the mankind making
Bird beast and flower
Fathering and all humbling darkness
Tells with silence the last light breaking
And the still hour
Is come of the sea tumbling in harness

And I must enter again the round
Zion of the water bead
And the synagogue of the ear of corn
Shall I let pray the shadow of a sound
Or sow my salt seed
In the least valley of sackcloth to mourn

The majesty and burning of the child's death.
I shall not murder
The mankind of her going with a grave truth
Nor blaspheme down the stations of the breath
With any further
Elegy of innocence and youth.

Deep with the first dead lies London's daughter,
Robed in the long friends,
The grains beyond age, the dark veins of her mother,
Secret by the unmourning water
Of the riding Thames.
After the first death, there is no other.

Poem in October

It was my thirtieth year to heaven
Woke to my hearing from harbour and neighbour wood
   And the mussel pooled and the heron
       Priested shore
     The morning beckon
With water praying and call of seagull and rook
And the knock of sailing boats on the net webbed wall
   Myself to set foot
      That second
   In the still sleeping town and set forth.

My birthday began with the water-
Birds and the birds of the winged trees flying my name
   Above the farms and the white horses
      And I rose
     In rainy autumn
And walked abroad in a shower of all my days.
High tide and the heron dived when I took the road
   Over the border
      And the gates
   Of the town closed as the town awoke.

A springful of larks in a rolling
Cloud and the roadside bushes brimming with whistling
   Blackbirds and the sun of October
      Summery
     On the hill's shoulder,
Here were fond climates and sweet singers suddenly
Come in the morning where I wandered and listened
   To the rain wringing
      Wind blow cold
   In the wood faraway under me.

Pale rain over the dwindling harbour
And over the sea wet church the size of a snail
 With its horns through mist and the castle
   Brown as owls
 But all the gardens
Of spring and summer were blooming in the tall tales
Beyond the border and under the lark full cloud.
  There could I marvel
   My birthday
 Away but the weather turned around.

 It turned away from the blithe country
And down the other air and the blue altered sky
 Streamed again a wonder of summer
   With apples
  Pears and red currants
And I saw in the turning so clearly a child's
Forgotten mornings when he walked with his mother
  Through the parables
   Of sun light
 And the legends of the green chapels

 And the twice told fields of infancy
That his tears burned my cheeks and his heart moved in mine.
 These were the woods the river and sea
   Where a boy
  In the listening
Summertime of the dead whispered the truth of his joy
To the trees and the stones and the fish in the tide.
  And the mystery
   Sang alive
 Still in the water and singingbirds.

 And there could I marvel my birthday
Away but the weather turned around. And the true
 Joy of the long dead child sang burning
   In the sun.

It was my thirtieth
Year to heaven stood there then in the summer noon
Though the town below lay leaved with October blood.
  O may my heart's truth
   Still be sung
 On this high hill in a year's turning.

This Side of the Truth
(for Llewelyn)

This side of the truth,
You may not see, my son,
King of your blue eyes
In the blinding country of youth,
That all is undone,
Under the unminding skies,
Of innocence and guilt
Before you move to make
One gesture of the heart or head,
Is gathered and spilt
Into the winding dark
Like the dust of the dead.

Good and bad, two ways
Of moving about your death
By the grinding sea,
King of your heart in the blind days,
Blow away like breath,
Go crying through you and me
And the souls of all men
Into the innocent
Dark, and the guilty dark, and good
Death, and bad death, and then
In the last element
Fly like the stars' blood,

Like the sun's tears,
Like the moon's seed, rubbish
And fire, the flying rant
Of the sky, king of your six years.
And the wicked wish,
Down the beginning of plants
And animals and birds,

Water and light, the earth and sky,
Is cast before you move,
And all your deeds and words,
Each truth, each lie,
Die in unjudging love.

Love in the Asylum

A stranger has come
To share my room in the house not right in the head,
A girl mad as birds

Bolting the night of the door with her arm her plume.
Strait in the mazed bed
She deludes the heaven-proof house with entering clouds

Yet she deludes with walking the nightmarish room,
At large as the dead,
Or rides the imagined oceans of the male wards.

She has come possessed
Who admits the delusive light through the bouncing wall,
Possessed by the skies

She sleeps in the narrow trough yet she walks the dust
Yet raves at her will
On the madhouse boards worn thin by my walking tears.

And taken by light in her arms at long and dear last
I may without fail
Suffer the first vision that set fire to the stars.

The Hunchback in the Park

The hunchback in the park
A solitary mister
Propped between trees and water
From the opening of the garden lock
That lets the trees and water enter
Until the Sunday sombre bell at dark

Eating bread from a newspaper
Drinking water from the chained cup
That the children filled with gravel
In the fountain basin where I sailed my ship
Slept at night in a dog kennel
But nobody chained him up.

Like the park birds he came early
Like the water he sat down
And Mister they called Hey mister
The truant boys from the town
Running when he had heard them clearly
On out of sound

Past lake and rockery
Laughing when he shook his paper
Hunchbacked in mockery .
Through the loud zoo of the willow groves
Dodging the park keeper
With his stick that picked up leaves.

And the old dog sleeper
Alone between nurses and swans
While the boys among willows
Made the tigers jump out of their eyes
To roar on the rockery stones
And the groves were blue with sailors

Made all day until bell time
A woman figure without fault
Straight as a young elm
Straight and tall from his crooked bones
That she might stand in the night
After the locks and chains

All night in the unmade park
After the railings and shrubberies
The birds the grass the trees the lake
And the wild boys innocent as strawberries
Had followed the hunchback
To his kennel in the dark.

Into Her Lying Down Head

Into her lying down head
His enemies entered bed,
Under the encumbered eyelid,
Through the rippled drum of the hair-buried ear;
And Noah's rekindled now unkind dove
Flew man-bearing there.
Last night in a raping wave
Whales unreined from the green grave
In fountains of origin gave up their love,
Along her innocence glided
Juan aflame and savagely young King Lear,
Queen Catherine howling bare
And Samson drowned in his hair,
The colossal intimacies of silent
Once seen strangers or shades on a stair;
There the dark blade and wanton sighing her down
To a haycock couch and the scythes of his arms
Rode and whistled a hundred times
Before the crowing morning climbed;
Man was the burning England she was sleep-walking, and the
enamouring island
Made her limbs blind by luminous charms,
Sleep to a newborn sleep in a swaddling loin-leaf stroked and
sang
And his runaway beloved childlike laid in the acorned
sand.

There where a numberless tongue
Wound their room with a male moan,
  His faith around her flew undone
And darkness hung the walls with baskets of snakes,
A furnace-nostrilled column-membered
          Super-or-near man
          Resembling to her dulled sense
          The thief of adolescence,
Early imaginary half remembered
          Oceanic lover alone
Jealousy cannot forget for all her sakes,
          Made his bad bed in her good
          Night, and enjoyed as he would.
Crying, white gowned, from the middle moonlit stages
          Out to the tiered and hearing tide,
Close and far she announced the theft of the heart
In the taken body at many ages,
          Trespasser and broken bride
          Celebrating at her side
All blood-signed assailings and vanished marriages in which he
          had no lovely part
          Nor could share, for his pride, to the least
Mutter and foul wingbeat of the solemnizing nightpriest
Her holy unholy hours with the always anonymous beast.

Two sand grains together in bed,
Head to heaven-circling head,
Singly lie with the whole wide shore,
The covering sea their nightfall with no names;
And out of every domed and soil-based shell
One voice in chains declaims
The female, deadly, and male
Libidinous betrayal,
Golden dissolving under the water veil.
A she bird sleeping brittle by
Her lover's wings that fold to-morrow's flight,
Within the nested treefork
Sings to the treading hawk
Carrion, paradise, chirrup my bright yolk.
A blade of grass longs with the meadow,
A stone lies lost and locked in the lark-high hill.
Open as to the air to the naked shadow
O she lies alone and still,
Innocent between two wars,
With the incestuous secret brother in the seconds to
perpetuate the stars,
A man torn up mourns in the sole night.
And the second comers, the severers, the enemies from the
deep
Forgotten dark, rest their pulse and bury their dead in her
faithless sleep.

Deaths and Entrances

On almost the incendiary eve
  Of several near deaths,
When one at the great least of your best loved
  And always known must leave
Lions and fires of his flying breath,
  Of your immortal friends
Who'd raise the organs of the counted dust
  To shoot and sing your praise,
One who called deepest down shall hold his peace
  That cannot sink or cease
  Endlessly to his wound
In many married London's estranging grief.

On almost the incendiary eve
  When at your lips and keys,
Locking, unlocking, the murdered strangers weave,
  One who is most unknown,
Your polestar neighbour, sun of another street,
  Will dive up to his tears.
He'll bathe his raining blood in the male sea
  Who strode for your own dead
And wind his globe out of your water thread
  And load the throats of shells
  With every cry since light
Flashed first across his thunderclapping eyes.

On almost the incendiary eve
  Of deaths and entrances,
When near and strange wounded on London's waves
  Have sought your single grave,
One enemy, of many, who knows well
  Your heart is luminous
In the watched dark, quivering through locks and caves,
  Will pull the thunderbolts

To shut the sun, plunge, mount your darkened keys
   And sear just riders back,
   Until that one loved lease
Looms the last Samson of your zodiac.

A Winter's Tale

It is a winter's tale
That the snow blind twilight ferries over the lakes
And floating fields from the farm in the cup of the vales,
Gliding windless through the hand folded flakes,
The pale breath of cattle at the stealthy sail,

And the stars falling cold,
And the smell of hay in the snow, and the far owl
Warning among the folds, and the frozen hold
Flocked with the sheep white smoke of the farm house cowl
In the river wended vales where the tale was told.

Once when the world turned old
On a star of faith pure as the drifting bread,
As the food and flames of the snow, a man unrolled
The scrolls of fire that burned in his heart and head,
Torn and alone in a farm house in a fold

Of fields. And burning then
In his firelit island ringed by the winged snow
And the dung hills white as wool and the hen
Roosts sleeping chill till the flame of the cock crow
Combs through the mantled yards and the morning men

Stumble out with their spades,
The cattle stirring, the mousing cat stepping shy,
The puffed birds hopping and hunting, the milkmaids
Gentle in their clogs over the fallen sky,
And all the woken farm at its white trades,

He knelt, he wept, he prayed,
By the spit and the black pot in the log bright light
And the cup and the cut bread in the dancing shade,
In the muffled house, in the quick of night,
At the point of love, forsaken and afraid.

49

He knelt on the cold stones,
He wept from the crest of grief, he prayed to the veiled sky
May his hunger go howling on bare white bones
Past the statues of the stables and the sky roofed sties
And the duck pond glass and the blinding byres alone

Into the home of prayers
And fires where he should prowl down the cloud
Of his snow blind love and rush in the white lairs.
His naked need struck him howling and bowed
Though no sound flowed down the hand folded air

But only the wind strung
Hunger of birds in the fields of the bread of water, tossed
In high corn and the harvest melting on their tongues.
And his nameless need bound him burning and lost
When cold as snow he should run the wended vales among

The rivers mouthed in night,
And drown in the drifts of his need, and lie curled caught
In the always desiring centre of the white
Inhuman cradle and the bride bed forever sought
By the believer lost and the hurled outcast of light.

Deliver him, he cried,
By losing him all in love, and cast his need
Alone and naked in the engulfing bride,
Never to flourish in the fields of the white seed
Or flower under the time dying flesh astride.

Listen. The minstrels sing
In the departed villages. The nightingale,
Dust in the buried wood, flies on the grains of her wings
And spells on the winds of the dead his winter's tale.
The voice of the dust of water from the withered spring

Is telling. The wizened
Stream with bells and baying water bounds. The dew rings
On the gristed leaves and the long gone glistening

Parish of snow. The carved mouths in the rock are wind swept
    strings.
Time sings through the intricately dead snow drop. Listen.

        It was a hand or sound
In the long ago land that glided the dark door wide
And there outside on the bread of the ground
A she bird rose and rayed like a burning bride.
A she bird dawned, and her breast with snow and scarlet
    downed.

        Look. And the dancers move
On the departed, snow bushed green, wanton in moon light
As a dust of pigeons. Exulting, the grave hooved
Horses, centaur dead, turn and tread the drenched white
Paddocks in the farms of birds. The dead oak walks for love.

        The carved limbs in the rock
Leap, as to trumpets. Calligraphy of the old
Leaves is dancing. Lines of age on the stones weave in a flock.
And the harp shaped voice of the water's dust plucks in a fold
Of fields. For love, the long ago she bird rises. Look.

        And the wild wings were raised
Above her folded head, and the soft feathered voice
Was flying through the house as though the she bird praised
And all the elements of the slow fall rejoiced
That a man knelt alone in the cup of the vales,

        In the mantle and calm,
By the spit and the black pot in the log bright light.
And the sky of birds in the plumed voice charmed
Him up and he ran like a wind after the kindling flight
Past the blind barns and byres of the windless farm.

        In the poles of the year
When black birds died like priests in the cloaked hedge row
And over the cloth of counties the far hills rode near,

Under the one leaved trees ran a scarecrow of snow
And fast through the drifts of the thickets antlered like deer,

Rags and prayers down the knee-
Deep hillocks and loud on the numbed lakes,
All night lost and long wading in the wake of the she-
Bird through the times and lands and tribes of the slow flakes.
Listen and look where she sails the goose plucked sea,

The sky, the bird, the bride,
The cloud, the need, the planted stars, the joy beyond
The fields of seed and the time dying flesh astride,
The heavens, the heaven, the grave, the burning font.
In the far ago land the door of his death glided wide,

And the bird descended.
On a bread white hill over the cupped farm
And the lakes and floating fields and the river wended
Vales where he prayed to come to the last harm
And the home of prayers and fires, the tale ended.

The dancing perishes
On the white, no longer growing green, and, minstrel dead,
The singing breaks in the snow shoed villages of wishes
That once cut the figures of birds on the deep bread
And over the glazed lakes skated the shapes of fishes

Flying. The rite is shorn
Of nightingale and centaur dead horse. The springs wither
Back. Lines of age sleep on the stones till trumpeting dawn.
Exultation lies down. Time buries the spring weather
That belled and bounded with the fossil and the dew reborn.

For the bird lay bedded
In a choir of wings, as though she slept or died,
And the wings glided wide and he was hymned and wedded,
And through the thighs of the engulfing bride,
The woman breasted and the heaven headed

        Bird, he was brought low,
Burning in the bride bed of love, in the whirl-
Pool at the wanting centre, in the folds
Of paradise, in the spun bud of the world.
And she rose with him flowering in her melting snow.

There Was a Saviour

There was a saviour
Rarer than radium,
Commoner than water, crueller than truth;
Children kept from the sun
Assembled at his tongue
To hear the golden note turn in a groove,
Prisoners of wishes locked their eyes
In the jails and studies of his keyless smiles.

The voice of children says
From a lost wilderness
There was calm to be done in his safe unrest,
When hindering man hurt
Man, animal, or bird
We hid our fears in that murdering breath,
Silence, silence to do, when earth grew loud,
In lairs and asylums of the tremendous shout.

There was glory to hear
In the churches of his tears,
Under his downy arm you sighed as he struck,
O you who could not cry
On to the ground when a man died
Put a tear for joy in the unearthly flood
And laid your cheek against a cloud-formed shell:
Now in the dark there is only yourself and myself.

Two proud, blacked brothers cry,
Winter-locked side by side,
To this inhospitable hollow year,
O we who could not stir
One lean sigh when we heard
Greed on man beating near and fire neighbour

But wailed and nested in the sky-blue wall
Now break a giant tear for the little known fall,

For the drooping of homes
That did not nurse our bones,
Brave deaths of only ones but never found,
Now see, alone in us,
Our own true strangers' dust
Ride through the doors of our unentered house.
Exiled in us we arouse the soft,
Unclenched, armless, silk and rough love that breaks all rocks.

In My Craft or Sullen Art

In my craft or sullen art
Exercised in the still night
When only the moon rages
And the lovers lie abed
With all their griefs in their arms,
I labour by singing light
Not for ambition or bread
Or the strut and trade of charms
On the ivory stages
But for the common wages
Of their most secret heart.

Not for the proud man apart
From the raging moon I write
On these spindrift pages
Nor for the towering dead
With their nightingales and psalms
But for the lovers, their arms
Round the griefs of the ages,
Who pay no praise or wages
Nor heed my craft or art.

Ceremony After a Fire Raid

Myselves
The grievers
Grieve
Among the street burned to tireless death
A child of a few hours
With its kneading mouth
Charred on the black breast of the grave
The mother dug, and its arms full of fires.

Begin
With singing
Sing
Darkness kindled back into beginning
When the caught tongue nodded blind,
A star was broken
Into the centuries of the child
Myselves grieve now, and miracles cannot atone.

Forgive
Us forgive
Us your death that myselves the believers
May hold it in a great flood
Till the blood shall spurt,
And the dust shall sing like a bird
As the grains blow, as your death grows, through our heart.

Crying
Your dying
Cry,
Child beyond cockcrow, by the fire-dwarfed
Street we chant the flying sea
In the body bereft.

Love is the last light spoken. Oh
Seed of sons in the loin of the black husk left.

II

I know not whether
Adam or Eve, the adorned holy bullock
Or the white ewe lamb
Or the chosen virgin
Laid in her snow
On the altar of London,
Was the first to die
In the cinder of the little skull,
O bride and bride groom
O Adam and Eve together
Lying in the lull
Under the sad breast of the head stone
White as the skeleton
Of the garden of Eden.

I know the legend
Of Adam and Eve is never for a second
Silent in my service
Over the dead infants
Over the one
Child who was priest and servants,
Word, singers, and tongue
In the cinder of the little skull,
Who was the serpent's
Night fall and the fruit like a sun,
Man and woman undone,
Beginning crumbled back to darkness
Bare as the nurseries
Of the garden of wilderness.

Into the organpipes and steeples
Of the luminous cathedrals,
Into the weathercocks' molten mouths
Rippling in twelve-winded circles,
Into the dead clock burning the hour
Over the urn of sabbaths
Over the whirling ditch of daybreak
Over the sun's hovel and the slum of fire
And the golden pavements laid in requiems,
Into the bread in a wheatfield of flames,
Into the wine burning like brandy,
The masses of the sea
The masses of the sea under
The masses of the infant-bearing sea
Erupt, fountain, and enter to utter for ever
Glory glory glory
The sundering ultimate kingdom of genesis' thunder.

Among Those Killed in the Dawn Raid
Was a Man Aged a Hundred

When the morning was waking over the war
He put on his clothes and stepped out and he died,
The locks yawned loose and a blast blew them wide,
He dropped where he loved on the burst pavement stone
And the funeral grains of the slaughtered floor.
Tell his street on its back he stopped a sun
And the craters of his eyes grew springshoots and fire
When all the keys shot from the locks, and rang.
Dig no more for the chains of his grey-haired heart.
The heavenly ambulance drawn by a wound
Assembling waits for the spade's ring on the cage.
O keep his bones away from that common cart,
The morning is flying on the wings of his age
And a hundred storks perch on the sun's right hand.

Fern Hill

Now as I was young and easy under the apple boughs
About the lilting house and happy as the grass was green,
    The night above the dingle starry,
        Time let me hail and climb
    Golden in the heydays of his eyes,
And honoured among wagons I was prince of the apple towns
And once below a time I lordly had the trees and leaves
        Trail with daisies and barley
    Down the rivers of the windfall light.

And as I was green and carefree, famous among the barns
About the happy yard and singing as the farm was home,
    In the sun that is young once only,
        Time let me play and be
    Golden in the mercy of his means,
And green and golden I was huntsman and herdsman, the calves
Sang to my horn, the foxes on the hills barked clear and cold,
        And the sabbath rang slowly
    In the pebbles of the holy streams.

All the sun long it was running, it was lovely, the hay
Fields high as the house, the tunes from the chimney, it was air
    And playing, lovely and watery
        And fire green as grass.
    And nightly under the simple stars
As I rode to sleep the owls were bearing the farm away,
All the moon long I heard, blessed among stables, the nightjars
        Flying with the ricks, and the horses
            Flashing into the dark.

And then to awake, and the farm, like a wanderer white
With the dew, come back, the cock on his shoulder: it was all
    Shining, it was Adam and maiden,
        The sky gathered again

And the sun grew round that very day.
So it must have been after the birth of the simple light
In the first, spinning place, the spellbound horses walking warm
 Out of the whinnying green stable
  On to the fields of praise.

And honoured among foxes and pheasants by the gay house
Under the new made clouds and happy as the heart was long,
 In the sun born over and over,
  I ran my heedless ways,
 My wishes raced through the house high hay
And nothing I cared, at my sky blue trades, that time allows
In all his tuneful turning so few and such morning songs
 Before the children green and golden
  Follow him out of grace,

Nothing I cared, in the lamb white days, that time would take me
Up to the swallow thronged loft by the shadow of my hand,
 In the moon that is always rising,
  Nor that riding to sleep
 I should hear him fly with the high fields
And wake to the farm forever fled from the childless land.
Oh as I was young and easy in the mercy of his means,
  Time held me green and dying
 Though I sang in my chains like the sea.

Poem on His Birthday

In the mustardseed sun,
By full tilt river and switchback sea
   Where the cormorants scud,
In his house on stilts high among beaks
   And palavers of birds
This sandgrain day in the bent bay's grave
   He celebrates and spurns
His driftwood thirty-fifth wind turned age;
   Herons spire and spear.

Under and round him go
Flounders, gulls, on their cold, dying trails,
   Doing what they are told,
Curlews aloud in the congered waves
   Work at their ways to death,
And the rhymer in the long tongued room,
   Who tolls his birthday bell,
Toils towards the ambush of his wounds;
   Herons, steeple stemmed, bless.

In the thistledown fall,
He sings towards anguish; finches fly
   In the claw tracks of hawks
On a seizing sky; small fishes glide
   Through wynds and shells of drowned
Ship towns to pastures of otters. He
   In his slant, racking house
And the hewn coils of his trade perceives
   Herons walk in their shroud,

The livelong river's robe
Of minnows wreathing around their prayer;
   And far at sea he knows,
Who slaves to his crouched, eternal end

Under a serpent cloud,
Dolphins dive in their turnturtle dust,
  The rippled seals streak down
To kill and their own tide daubing blood
  Slides good in the sleek mouth.

  In a cavernous, swung
Wave's silence, wept white angelus knells.
  Thirty-five bells sing struck
On skull and scar where his loves lie wrecked,
  Steered by the falling stars.
And to-morrow weeps in a blind cage
  Terror will rage apart
Before chains break to a hammer flame
  And love unbolts the dark

  And freely he goes lost
In the unknown, famous light of great
  And fabulous, dear God.
Dark is a way and light is a place,
  Heaven that never was
Nor will be ever is always true,
  And, in that brambled void,
Plenty as blackberries in the woods
  The dead grow for His joy.

  There he might wander bare
With the spirits of the horseshoe bay
  Or the stars' seashore dead,
Marrow of eagles, the roots of whales
  And wishbones of wild geese,
With blessed, unborn God and His Ghost,
  And every soul His priest,
Gulled and chanter in young Heaven's fold
  Be at cloud quaking peace,

  But dark is a long way.
He, on the earth of the night, alone

With all the living, prays,
Who knows the rocketing wind will blow
    The bones out of the hills,
And the scythed boulders bleed, and the last
    Rage shattered waters kick
Masts and fishes to the still quick stars,
    Faithlessly unto Him

Who is the light of old
And air shaped Heaven where souls grow wild
    As horses in the foam:
Oh, let me midlife mourn by the shrined
    And druid herons' vows
The voyage to ruin I must run,
    Dawn ships clouted aground,
Yet, though I cry with tumbledown tongue,
    Count my blessings aloud:

Four elements and five
Senses, and man a spirit in love
    Tangling through this spun slime
To his nimbus bell cool kingdom come
    And the lost, moonshine domes,
And the sea that hides his secret selves
    Deep in its black, base bones,
Lulling of spheres in the seashell flesh,
    And this last blessing most,

That the closer I move
To death, one man through his sundered hulks,
    The louder the sun blooms
And the tusked, ramshackling sea exults;
    And every wave of the way
And gale I tackle, the whole world then,
    With more triumphant faith
Than ever was since the world was said,
    Spins its morning of praise,

I hear the bouncing hills
Grow larked and greener at berry brown
   Fall and the dew larks sing
Taller this thunderclap spring, and how
   More spanned with angels ride
The mansouled fiery islands! Oh,
   Holier then their eyes,
And my shining men no more alone
   As I sail out to die.

Do Not Go Gentle into that Good Night

Do not go gentle into that good night,
Old age should burn and rave at close of day;
Rage, rage against the dying of the light.

Though wise men at their end know dark is right,
Because their words had forked no lightning they
Do not go gentle into that good night.

Good men, the last wave by, crying how bright
Their frail deeds might have danced in a green bay,
Rage, rage against the dying of the light.

Wild men who caught and sang the sun in flight,
And learn, too late, they grieved it on its way,
Do not go gentle into that good night.

Grave men, near death, who see with blinding sight
Blind eyes could blaze like meteors and be gay,
Rage, rage against the dying of the light.

And you, my father, there on the sad height,
Curse, bless, me now with your fierce tears, I pray.
Do not go gentle into that good night.
Rage, rage against the dying of the light.

Lament

When I was a windy boy and a bit
And the black spit of the chapel fold,
(Sighed the old ram rod, dying of women),
I tiptoed shy in the gooseberry wood,
The rude owl cried like a telltale tit,
I skipped in a blush as the big girls rolled
Ninepin down on the donkeys' common,
And on seesaw sunday nights I wooed
Whoever I would with my wicked eyes,
The whole of the moon I could love and leave
All the green leaved little weddings' wives
In the coal black bush and let them grieve.

When I was a gusty man and a half
And the black beast of the beetles' pews,
(Sighed the old ram rod, dying of bitches),
Not a boy and a bit in the wick-
Dipping moon and drunk as a new dropped calf,
I whistled all night in the twisted flues,
Midwives grew in the midnight ditches,
And the sizzling beds of the town cried, Quick! –
Whenever I dove in a breast high shoal,
Wherever I ramped in the clover quilts,
Whatsoever I did in the coal-
Black night, I left my quivering prints.

When I was a man you could call a man
And the black cross of the holy house,
(Sighed the old ram rod, dying of welcome),
Brandy and ripe in my bright, bass prime,
No springtailed tom in the red hot town
With every simmering woman his mouse
But a hillocky bull in the swelter
Of summer come in his great good time

To the sultry, biding herds, I said,
Oh, time enough when the blood creeps cold,
And I lie down but to sleep in bed,
For my sulking, skulking, coal black soul!

When I was a half of the man I was
And serve me right as the preachers warn,
(Sighed the old ram rod, dying of downfall),
No flailing calf or cat in a flame
Or hickory bull in milky grass
But a black sheep with a crumpled horn,
At last the soul from its foul mousehole
Slung pouting out when the limp time came;
And I gave my soul a blind, slashed eye,
Gristle and rind, and a roarers' life,
And I shoved it into the coal black sky
To find a woman's soul for a wife.

Now I am a man no more no more
And a black reward for a roaring life,
(Sighed the old ram rod, dying of strangers),
Tidy and cursed in my dove cooed room
I lie down thin and hear the good bells jaw –
For, oh, my soul found a sunday wife
In the coal black sky and she bore angels!
Harpies around me out of her womb!
Chastity prays for me, piety sings,
Innocence sweetens my last black breath,
Modesty hides my thighs in her wings,
And all the deadly virtues plague my death!

In Country Sleep

I

Never and never, my girl riding far and near
In the land of the hearthstone tales, and spelled asleep,
Fear or believe that the wolf in a sheepwhite hood
Loping and bleating roughly and blithely shall leap,
                                        My dear, my dear,
Out of a lair in the flocked leaves in the dew dipped year
To eat your heart in the house in the rosy wood.

Sleep, good, for ever, slow and deep, spelled rare and wise,
My girl ranging the night in the rose and shire
Of the hobnail tales: no gooseherd or swine will turn
Into a homestall king or hamlet of fire
                                        And prince of ice
To court the honeyed heart from your side before sunrise
In a spinney of ringed boys and ganders, spike and burn,

Nor the innocent lie in the rooting dingle wooed
And staved, and riven among plumes my rider weep.
From the broomed witch's spume you are shielded by fern
And flower of country sleep and the greenwood keep.
                                        Lie fast and soothed,
Safe be and smooth from the bellows of the rushy brood.
Never, my girl, until tolled to sleep by the stern

Bell believe or fear that the rustic shade or spell
Shall harrow and snow the blood while you ride wide and near,
For who unmanningly haunts the mountain ravened eaves
Or skulks in the dell moon but moonshine echoing clear
                                        From the starred well?
A hill touches an angel! Out of a saint's cell
The nightbird lauds through nunneries and domes of leaves

Her robin breasted tree, three Marys in the rays.
Sanctum sanctorum the animal eye of the wood
In the rain telling its beads, and the gravest ghost
The owl at its knelling. Fox and holt kneel before blood.
                              Now the tales praise
The star rise at pasture and nightlong the fables graze
On the lord's-table of the bowing grass. Fear most

For ever of all not the wolf in his baaing hood
Nor the tusked prince, in the ruttish farm, at the rind
And mire of love, but the Thief as meek as the dew.
The country is holy: O bide in that country kind,
                              Know the green good,
Under the prayer wheeling moon in the rosy wood
Be shielded by chant and flower and gay may you

Lie in grace. Sleep spelled at rest in the lowly house
In the squirrel nimble grove, under linen and thatch
And star: held and blessed, though you scour the high four
Winds, from the dousing shade and the roarer at the latch,
                              Cool in your vows.
Yet out of the beaked, web dark and the pouncing boughs
Be you sure the Thief will seek a way sly and sure

And sly as snow and meek as dew blown to the thorn,
This night and each vast night until the stern bell talks
In the tower and tolls to sleep over the stalls
Of the hearthstone tales my own, lost love; and the soul walks
                              The waters shorn.
This night and each night since the falling star you were born,
Ever and ever he finds a way, as the snow falls,

As the rain falls, hail on the fleece, as the vale mist rides
Through the haygold stalls, as the dew falls on the wind-
Milled dust of the apple tree and the pounded islands
Of the morning leaves, as the star falls, as the winged
                              Apple seed glides,

And falls, and flowers in the yawning wound at our sides,
As the world falls, silent as the cyclone of silence.

II

Night and the reindeer on the clouds above the haycocks
And the wings of the great roc ribboned for the fair!
The leaping saga of prayer! And high, there, on the hare-
                              Heeled winds the rooks
Cawing from their black bethels soaring, the holy books
Of birds! Among the cocks like fire the red fox

Burning! Night and the vein of birds in the winged, sloe wrist
Of the wood! Pastoral beat of blood through the laced leaves!
The stream from the priest black wristed spinney and sleeves
                              Of thistling frost
Of the nightingale's din and tale! The upgiven ghost
Of the dingle torn to singing and the surpliced

Hill of cypresses! The din and tale in the skimmed
Yard of the buttermilk rain on the pail! The sermon
Of blood! The bird loud vein! The saga from mermen
                              To seraphim
Leaping! The gospel rooks! All tell, this night, of him
Who comes as red as the fox and sly as the heeled wind.

Illumination of music! the lulled black-backed
Gull, on the wave with sand in its eyes! And the foal moves
Through the shaken greensward lake, silent, on moonshod
   hooves,
                              In the winds' wakes.
Music of elements, that a miracle makes!
Earth, air, water, fire, singing into the white act,

The haygold haired, my love asleep, and the rift blue
Eyed, in the haloed house, in her rareness and hilly
High riding, held and blessed and true, and so stilly
                              Lying the sky

Might cross its planets, the bell weep, night gather her eyes,
The Thief fall on the dead like the willy nilly dew,

Only for the turning of the earth in her holy
Heart! Slyly, slowly, hearing the wound in her side go
Round the sun, he comes to my love like the designed snow,
                                        And truly he
Flows to the strand of flowers like the dew's ruly sea,
And surely he sails like the ship shape clouds. Oh he

Comes designed to my love to steal not her tide raking
Wound, nor her riding high, nor her eyes, nor kindled hair,
But her faith that each vast night and the saga of prayer
                                        He comes to take
Her faith that this last night for his unsacred sake
He comes to leave her in the lawless sun awaking

Naked and forsaken to grieve he will not come.
Ever and ever by all your vows believe and fear
My dear this night he comes and night without end my dear
                                        Since you were born:
And you shall wake, from country sleep, this dawn and each
    first dawn,
Your faith as deathless as the outcry of the ruled sun.

Over Sir John's Hill

Over Sir John's hill,
The hawk on fire hangs still;
In a hoisted cloud, at drop of dusk, he pulls to his claws
And gallows, up the rays of his eyes the small birds of the bay
And the shrill child's play
Wars
Of the sparrows and such who swansing, dusk, in wrangling
   hedges.
And blithely they squawk
To fiery tyburn over the wrestle of elms until
The flash the noosed hawk
Crashes, and slowly the fishing holy stalking heron
In the river Towy below bows his tilted headstone.

Flash, and the plumes crack,
And a black cap of jack-
Daws Sir John's just hill dons, and again the gulled birds hare
To the hawk on fire, the halter height, over Towy's fins,
In a whack of wind.
There
Where the elegiac fisherbird stabs and paddles
In the pebbly dab-filled
Shallow and sedge, and 'dilly dilly,' calls the loft hawk,
'Come and be killed,'
I open the leaves of the water at a passage
Of psalms and shadows among the pincered sandcrabs
   prancing

And read, in a shell,
Death clear as a buoy's bell:
All praise of the hawk on fire in hawk-eyed dusk be sung,
When his viperish fuse hangs looped with flames under the
   brand
Wing, and blest shall

Young
Green chickens of the bay and bushes cluck, 'dilly, dilly,
Come let us die.'
We grieve as the blithe birds, never again, leave shingle and
   elm,
The heron and I,
I young Aesop fabling to the near night by the dingle
Of eels, saint heron hymning in the shell-hung distant

Crystal harbour vale
Where the sea cobbles sail,
And wharves of water where the walls dance and the white
   cranes stilt.
It is the heron and I, under judging Sir John's elmed
Hill, tell-tale the knelled
Guilt
Of the led-astray birds whom God, for their breast of whistles,
Have mercy on,
God in his whirlwind silence save, who marks the sparrows
   hail,
For their souls' song.
Now the heron grieves in the weeded verge. Through windows
Of dusk and water I see the tilting whispering

Heron, mirrored, go,
As the snapt feathers snow,
Fishing in the tear of the Towy. Only a hoot owl
Hollows, a grassblade blown in cupped hands, in the looted
   elms
And no green cocks or hens
Shout
Now on Sir John's hill. The heron, ankling the scaly
Lowlands of the waves,
Makes all the music; and I who hear the tune of the slow,
Wear-willow river, grave,
Before the lunge of the night, the notes on this time-shaken
Stone for the sake of the souls of the slain birds sailing.

In the White Giant's Thigh

Through throats where many rivers meet, the curlews cry,
Under the conceiving moon, on the high chalk hill,
And there this night I walk in the white giant's thigh
Where barren as boulders women lie longing still

To labour and love though they lay down long ago.

Through throats where many rivers meet, the women pray,
Pleading in the waded bay for the seed to flow
Though the names on their weed grown stones are rained away,

And alone in the night's eternal, curving act
They yearn with tongues of curlews for the unconceived
And immemorial sons of the cudgelling, hacked

Hill. Who once in gooseskin winter loved all ice leaved
In the courters' lanes, or twined in the ox roasting sun
In the wains tonned so high that the wisps of the hay
Clung to the pitching clouds, or gay with any one
Young as they in the after milking moonlight lay

Under the lighted shapes of faith and their moonshade
Petticoats galed high, or shy with the rough riding boys,
Now clasp me to their grains in the gigantic glade,

Who once, green countries since, were a hedgerow of joys.
Time by, their dust was flesh the swineherd rooted sly,
Flared in the reek of the wiving sty with the rush
Light of his thighs, spreadeagle to the dunghill sky,
Or with their orchard man in the core of the sun's bush
Rough as cows' tongues and thrashed with brambles their
    buttermilk
Manes, under his quenchless summer barbed gold to the bone,

Or rippling soft in the spinney moon as the silk
And ducked and draked white lake that harps to a hail stone.

Who once were a bloom of wayside brides in the hawed house
And heard the lewd, wooed field flow to the coming frost,
The scurrying, furred small friars squeal, in the dowse
Of day, in the thistle aisles, till the white owl crossed

Their breast, the vaulting does roister, the horned bucks climb
Quick in the wood at love, where a torch of foxes foams,
All birds and beasts of the linked night uproar and chime

And the mole snout blunt under his pilgrimage of domes,
Or, butter fat goosegirls, bounced in a gambo bed,
Their breasts full of honey, under their gander king
Trounced by his wings in the hissing shippen, long dead
And gone that barley dark where their clogs danced in the
    spring,
And their firefly hairpins flew, and the ricks ran round –

(But nothing bore, no mouthing babe to the veined hives
Hugged, and barren and bare on Mother Goose's ground
They with the simple Jacks were a boulder of wives) –

Now curlew cry me down to kiss the mouths of their dust.

The dust of their kettles and clocks swings to and fro
Where the hay rides now or the bracken kitchens rust
As the arc of the billhooks that flashed the hedges low
And cut the birds' boughs that the minstrel sap ran red.
They from houses where the harvest kneels, hold me hard,
Who heard the tall bell sail down the Sundays of the dead
And the rain wring out its tongues on the faded yard,
Teach me the love that is evergreen after the fall leaved
Grave, after Belovéd on the grass gulfed cross is scrubbed
Off by the sun and Daughters no longer grieved
Save by their long desirers in the fox cubbed
Streets or hungering in the crumbled wood: to these
Hale dead and deathless do the women of the hill
Love for ever meridian through the courters' trees

And the daughters of darkness flame like Fawkes fires still.